Running, lightwave riding

By Allison Grayhurst

Table of Contents

The Letting Go

I
Blast

Blast your devil's heart,
make it into paper confetti,
take it into outer space
and leave it there.
You stood on my shoes as I was
wearing them, dug your heels in
and spat in my eyes.
Cruel corpse rising from a muddy grave,
you are weak and monstrous, always claiming
to be the victim of someone else's scheme.
You are madness, the sharp ridged knife
of madness flaying in chaotic whiplash
at the sky, the birds, and all manner of trees.
Take back your darkness, swallow it whole,
let it stew in your innards, ruminate, reuniting
with the depravity already there.
You will never lie to me again,
pretending you wanted love when all you wanted
was to spread your malignancy, vengeance
for an imagined wrong, to give a landing slap
with the full force of violent resentment and envy.
Slither away, your bite left no mark, ineffectual
as your attempts to love. Judas, Brutus, master
of deep, un-emerge-able hell. Go home. Blast away
your caked-on body filth, reductive stench, spoiling
all you claimed to hold sacred.

II
Scapegoat

Give yourself over
to the burn on your back,
the sordid array of demons
counselling your thoughts.
Let loose the bell string,
pull hard and hard again.
Find yourself a ditch to
fall into, scream out of,
wailing at the stars.
Ruin a good morning with
your sticky filth, throwing blame
to deflect from the wounds of
your own weakness.

I add you up - here, here and here.
I will not play along
with your parlour-tricks, your mayhem
of pointing-the-finger lies
when what I gave was love
- not perfect - but love nonetheless.

Coil up in your bitterness, resentments you wear
like a special pair of shoes,
walking around, leaving prints over prints
of your relentless pointless pacing.
I am not who you think I am, not willing
to hold guilt for your depravity, for a crime never my own.
I will say it again - I loved - I gave you love
the best I knew how, and I showed kindness.

Give yourself over to the intercourse
of false justifications and accusations and
see how it feels to be alone, here,
with what is left -
broken dollar-store jewelry, dandruff flakes.
Give yourself over and
get lost,
out of my thoughts
out into the isolated frozen-dead terrain
of your own sick making.

III
Monster

Surrender to restore
the gifted strength, bruised
by curses, but otherwise unharmed.
Lay down the cloak of justice,
Achilles' revenge. Shout fire!
and let it burn.
What I did was falter,
overspeak with heart-felt enthusiasm,
that is all - thinking it was to a friend,
when in fact it was a snake, no, a worm,
without backbone, fangs or face.
Pour salt on it, watch it dissolve
into its true slime-form, formless
as the excuses of Brutus who cared nothing
for Rome, for Caesar, had only his own
power-grab in mind, wounded
that he was not chosen, pride-puffed,
feigning altruism to self-justify
his ruthless deed.
Appear to me, then pass like a bad smell
when a window is opened, or lavender calm is sprayed.
I was fooled when I should have honoured
the signs before, left, when I first witnessed
your shadow-flood self-pity play. Then
I should have hung up the phone and never
called back. But I kept on, over that hurdle, ignoring
its truth, always wondering, waiting for the monster
to unmask again. When it did, it was worse than before.

The wolves of hell have you now, surrounded
on all dimensional sides. Your vicious tongue,
still twisting and twirling, angered at the glare of the sun.
        Promise me never to return. I promise you
I have walked by you, looked, then walked
further up the devil's back, out
of the inverted pit of your doing, never to look again.
        Know I have no good memories of you,
they have all been eradicated by this hideous calamity.
Your words of love ring like lies,
hiding a hostile, grudge-madness,
a decade of trust mutilated by spiritual sickness.
        Know your hydra head is now exposed,
sliced off, cauterised, nullified at the core, illusion blown -
your sweet-honey-poison dried up, disposed.

IV
Deviant

Diminished in love
by excessive self-pity, locked
in anguish, in anger, in the burn-machine
lake layer of hell
as the long sword of your insanity
is wielded, intending to split
my skull in two.

I felt it breeze past, just missing its mark.
I felt the shock as I swerved, as you
suckled on the teat of your unfounded
resentments, brewing for months, draped
in pretty fabric, niceties and endearments.
How long had your soul gone foul,
and I never noticed?
No discussion, just your rigid arthritic finger
pointing, your creased forehead further creasing,
corpse-like and rising like a poltergeist
from the boiling mire.

Poor soul. Poor you as all of your
bold spiritual proclamations are reduced to naught.
Take care old woman. You cannot create
or be uplifted tied to this abhorrent deformity
of deluded self-righteousness.

You can feel good for a second, lift your sword,
and be exhilarated. You can rub your hands together,
feel the power of cruelty, demolishing

a friendship with one swift cut.
You can and you did, and it is now done -

The cancer I never knew was there is removed,
every cell radiated and eradicated.
I proclaim gratitude for getting me out,
for releasing me from the leach tethered to my underbelly,
masquerading as a trusted alley.

I see you, your collected violent distortions, the rage
you assume, your sword in its ruthless downward assault,
swing, strike past, dark mass amputated, and I am set free.

V
The Hollow

The burn was received, betrayal
like a thousand strikes
on the same spot - ripping off
first my skin, then sinews.
A burn like a confession of hate,
masquerading for years as love.

That side has now descended, into the hollow,
along with all that burns and whose heat
cannot be tamed or reconciled.
I put a steel sheet over that hollow,
cover it for good and breathe easy in my escape,
tie my hair back and sing loudly with
my joy and intellect intact - with my trust in
God unharmed, my language rejuvenated.

Layers of arsenal fumes, rising,
I see you below in that hollow
hunched over, lamenting
a sickly self-pitying cry.
Already your hands and arms, up to your elbows,
buried like stakes deep in the unforgiving ground.
You cannot move. You cannot hope for better days.
Your hissing is useless, and the venom from your lips
dissipates into nothing as it leaves your gaping mouth.
You, stuck in a frozen mire, cut off
from the current, condensed, calcified, and stalled,
with only your conceit, your woe-is-me!
to give you voice, some
semblance of rudimentary comfort.

Egg

Periwinkle garden,
flowers folded
into a dumpling.

I sit on the bottom floor
of a blessing
before it builds and blooms,
before its face has distinction,
expression, perfect individuality.

Low ache of forming,
wandering cold plains, over icy lakes
through dead forests and caves.

Almost ripe,
platelets connecting, composing
a singular solid substance. Then

out of the egg and into the vast ocean,
forward, shell collapsing, imploding, out
free-riding, embodying
a fully sufficient infant form.

Child

The child twists a ringlet,
runs to the shops to buy
candy, rides her bike
by the river and assembles
a dream-world, bigger world
than her whole reality.
The child found worship in her heart
for God and love
for an infant raccoon alone under a tree,
talked to herself incessantly, and often,
she talked to God, and to his son, Jesus.
She went to school, but chalked it up
to unimportant servitude, felt joyful
and free, plucking the autumn leaves,
engaging with the neighbour's dog.
The child was wild, swinging
from willow branches, throwing stones,
skipping stones, toes always at the edge
of the unsettled river.
Cats were her guardians, confidants and kin.
Church was boredom, except for the one place
where the light was let in, that place
took over her full imagination
as she traveled through and into
an instinctual reverie.
The child loved her family,
was allowed every independence,
was ostracized by the other children
for her crocheted clothes and the colour
of her flaming hair. Some called her witch,

others, an atrocity, and the grown-ups, beautiful.
The child rode horses when she got older,
wrote down the songs of clouds and the names of
the crows that would follow her, converse with her
from the school bus window.
The child found her belonging in her own head,
with the animals, and sometimes, she remembers,
walking silently, holding the hand of a great angel.

Cage of Many Pockets and Layers

Lead,
into the land of vermin,
infesting the once blooming shores,
past the emergency-alarm, into
living fires, boiling and sharp in
their arrogant countenance.

Alone on a humble rock, standing -
arms folded, then stretched wide and up.
I take the hand and am led to a land
that tests my dignity and my resolve.
Many voices I must lose, people to leave behind.

The ship is the hand
leading through levels of horror
until the gate opens
to the possibility for redemption.

Wings of demons block the sky - pilgrimage eternal,
shaking off pity for the futile swarm moving
like lips of a mouth moving that offers no sound or groan.

My mind is tied to heaven, committed to resurgence.
My heart breaks but it is still whole, leaving,
being led over the land of naught, where there is plenty
of self-righteous indignation, self-sorrowing gleam
and the shadows,
led through and over
flailing limbs, bodies multiplying –
a thickening mass, swirling, swirling…

No grief, No madness

See yourself with real eyes,
there is no need for useless mythology.
The winter has come, the plants have died.
In spring they will take root and begin
to show promise. Just like you,
nothing magical –

You swell in times of joy
and deflate in times of sorrow,
stitching the inflatable boat.

This is your seat, accept it.
The struggle is the dream,
a hot order of suffering, unnecessary.

Stand up, kiss the Buddha and sit down.

Poet

My breath and blood,
my spiritual soldier,
death expresses itself
then ends to find another muse.
Hold me in your form,
unoffended, know I am
capable of true choice,
planting colours before unseen.

My last call, I am withdrawing,
weakening, biting a bitter morsel.
Darkness is a hymn, infiltrating
my subconscious.

I will take the globe and smash the sphere,
my boundless exemplary love, lover
of the embracing midnight, star light and roses.

I have no customs I am determined to keep.
I will give up all my rituals, my summer garden
to walk again, with you, on fire.

Monarchs

The monarchs begin their migration.
The souls of the deceased start to visit.
Temperance comes
with discipline, conviction
to not evade the truth or promises.

The last time I looked into your eyes
you were dying, trusting my love for you
and all the love that shielded around
your frail and fading body.
One year and I still miss you in my gut,
an emptiness that cannot be quelled.
This is the bird song, the emphasis
of individual brightness. The gift of you
and others too of gentle and lost natures.

The monarchs come to my back garden.
I greet them. I know each one -
their wing patterns, their flight patterns.
One day I will be a monarch,
a whiff of my soul, darting
from flower to flower, offering
a mild comfort to soothe
the pangs of vanished intimacies.

My love

I am still in awe
of the deep delight that
rises in your eyes
like a constellation surfaces
from the thick flesh of dark night
and sings to me - ethereal,
images pounding the back of my mind,
breaking through the wet cemented barrier,
sure to drown me, incorporate me into its own.

You are magic, a wilderness
tempered with spiritual intelligence where
your genius sits on a throne, high above the
primal ground, directing each disruption into
an exuberant harmony, changing the dull light
of chaos into a living ceremony, pulsing
and sensually tearing the seams
- heightened evolution -

my love,
my truest friendship, your power is beautiful.
It never wanes or falters. I love you still
like at the beginning
when we found a field and twirled
in joyful abandon, knowing what we found
and what was to come. It is coming
again, a future without waste or holding back.

Your rich glory raging like
a storm-tossed sea.
You are tied to the resting point.
You are tied to the gravity
of the moon. You spread your arms.
I watch you receive, and then
I will watch what enfolds.

Stand

I stood
where all things feared
were served with the promise
of this perpetual.

I stood
at half-mast,
my energy so recently
abundant, now draining, and
my hopes, mummified, soon
to be buried.

I stood and saw what I saw,
but it made no difference.
The light was inferior to this calamity.
Declarations came and went without execution.

I stood and said I would not go back,
but I did. I let the fruit spoil,
my own humanity overcome
with a ripe mix
of rage and despair.

I stood on a steep slope,
looking for
a soft grassy landing
or a way to stand
with equilibrium.

Visceral

The voice breaks down
into tiny fragments, each
filled with a unique harmony,
some clash in reckless bawls,
others fill with a steady fever.

The voice collects itself, gains frenzy
like a stallion no one could tame or mount.
The voice claims death, as even in death
it will not be defeated or subdued,
but will grow like waves in a storm, crash
and come back, rising, swallowing the shore
as it wakes.

The voice is a raging giant wanting fleshy dream,
rejecting limitations, leadership
from a reasoning baritone.

The voice outweighs imprisonment,
carnivorous oppression and the sighs
of consuming cancer.

The voice is tall
for its years.
The fabric it wears
is from the entrails of fate,
from the sinews of predictive design.

It has no cause and effect,
as it shouts out its riddle, its savage roar.

You can't confront it and win.
You can't pollute it with existential doubts.

It grips the universal jugular
with its teeth and claws,
digs in, utterly enjoying
the bloodied feast.

Sparrow

I see the spider dance, smoke
dancing on the edge of a scream.
I am that spider
dancing as I continue downstream.
Can I be a tree or a curvy vine?
Can I grow a cloud or just one
bulb flower?
Fated to be broken like all else
living on the Earth, soiled, striving, but always incomplete.
Can I trust enough to win back my soul?
Be immersed in the fog and still know the way?

My keeper, my mid-summer garden,
the bull shark is coming with the encroaching wave,
swimming will not be enough, not a floaty, not a raft
will stave off its violent power.
I will need something larger to fit on, something absolute
to cull this danger, an island on its own, a hand,
blessed and strong to raise me from the inevitable grave.

Your love is all I have ever known
when I know love. Pick me up with the rest of
the laundry you plan to clean - make light work of me,
set me down folded, refreshed,
ready to be worn. I am prepared to live
and I don't want to die
like a rusted vent, my metal
slowly corroding, crumbling until I am left without

grace, usefulness or substance. I don't want to walk
into the darkness again - the hollow of all hollows,
wailing with pain and rage and nakedness
in the burning coal fires.

I am your child. I am your sparrow, please
open the cage-latch, cup me as your own -
then let me go, and my freedom
will give you joy, will give you glory.

Blackout

If you knew
the fierce immersion,
tarnishing your already
dilapidated innards
would you have sunk so close to death,
your heart racing, aching with excruciating
escalation, skipping beats?
Would you have preoccupied your mind
with other people's good fortune, grow
bitter at your own failure to thrive,
and desired a dream that was never part
of your original vision?

You have one path and you must follow.
One that allows for no detours
or trips to sunny islands.
Faith is needed after the fall, before you land -
in the in-between time
when destruction feels inevitable, trust
there are arms to catch you, angels to guide you
gently to the ground, stand you upright
without permanent damage.
This faith is not a leap but happens
after you are pushed off the edge,
happens in the anticipation of disaster.

If you knew that was what was asked for
would you have let it retch up and slice
your essential organ like a pie?

Will you now, that you are recovering,
trust, as you are still falling, still facing
what seems like only-doom?

Will you relax into God's gracious love,
awaken a new level of faith that beats afresh
in spite of the rigid rocky terrain
fast approaching below?

I Stand Up

I stand up, everything
falls down, the load and the balance
on a soft bed of nothingness to catch
and embrace in a cruel dream
of freedom.
      I draw my breath in the rising wave,
knowing the calm waters are too lonely
for sustenance.
      This has butchered my means of survival,
drowning my body in acid-mud.
This has rounded out the edges, so
like a hard ball, I am tumbling down
an incline that stretches out
to a cliff with fast momentum,
no chance of halting or even slowing down.
      I found a piece of joy in day-to-day service
and must pay with blood flow, extreme heat and drought,
pay and never have a day without survival's worrisome
stranglehold gnawing out my intestines, making holes
here, serious as death, serious
as an asteroid breaking the atmosphere,
thinning my faith and all I hold sacred,
tying it down on a large rock, trying me up
on a large rock, in slow decomposition,
waiting the buzzard's peck and sting.

Veiled

The splendid vision
was announced then
denounced and the whole
inspiring fire fizzled invisible.

For decades, possessed,
but still able to protect the ones I love.
Yesterday and months before, the possession
lost its rule, the blood rage coiled inside of me cooled
but this open space created has taken away
my fight with it, and every ounce of security.

Concentrating on this stand-by whiff of hope,
hope as the thing practiced and opposite to struggling,
though not enough to fill my lungs with faith, not enough
to inhale a good breath or breathe at ease
before sleep.

I don't even know my name
anymore - my demons were never slain,
they just dissipated, taken by a ghostly victory
that I cannot claim as my own courage-doing
or as a song.

It is good that they are gone
but what they gave (food for survival)
is gone with them and I cannot see a way
forward, cannot see any secret that will feed this house
and stabilize it so I can live, clean the floor

and not wonder how long I can step here, step here
and hold the ones I love in safety.

The race is done though I never reached
the finish line. I was just plucked from the track
onto a sideroad without a knapsack or a spoon.
I can blow right through my fingers.
I can curl my toes but I cannot take a step,
not like this, deserted, helpless
at this bardo crossing.

Useless

This shelter is threadbare
like a low-battery flashlight,
barely making a dark corner visible.
I sang to find an easeful slumber.
I left my empty bin by the road,
begging for a refill.

Summer is behind me.
The grass is torn
from tiny claws and pecking.
I live below the breathing line
and there is no way to rise higher
or join a harmony to unfasten my chains.

Attempting flashing solutions in a frantic rush
trying for escape, but the land I stand on
is too hard to burrow under
and there are no trees to climb.

I wait for the door to open, knowing the door
is just a dream. That sickly feeling overflows
as each effort I make for freedom
deflates, fruitless, impotent.

Interchange - warm running

Open the stark and twisted plot,
then replenish it with a prize perfume,
everlasting, infiltrating with its veiled odour
as a mild but sublime soothing caress.

Dry up the stream that ran toxic
through the yard, dig the trench deeper
and build a river with a waterfall
pouring down, energized by power manifold.

Pull out the splinter that slipped close to bone,
for decades festering, bulging in a painful swell,
leave the wound to air and forget its throb.

Swim through the spectrum colours
that trapped you in their grip,
burst out of their array and be dazzled
on a hill, at a height triumphant, astounding.

The Spell was a Shield

The spell was a child
that fell from a high tree,
now broken, always
asleep. Blindfolded climbing
up a steep hill until I crossed
the pinnacle-edge and found myself laid
flat - a million fractures
puzzle-piecing my solidarity.
At the end of the labyrinth
into death's mocking jaws, swallowed
into the heartless chamber, crushed in very direction,
no soft resting spot, no treaties for equality or deliverance.

The spell has evaporated, and with it, false notions
of guarantees, help from others, every earthly
security I tied my lifeline to.
Thresholds were crossed
only to learn they were never there, just to
learn the Aquarius-light I was drinking from was
no light but a bitter detachment from reality, a lack
of understanding.

The spell is charred, taken away.
I am open now, and new and
ever so fragile without a path or protection.
Everything is air, and what isn't air is thin glass,
meaningless see-through enclosures, a false
blocking off of some things from other things,
a false truth destroyed with no truth left yet
to replace it.

Slap

Limpid dreams
removed with grand intervention,
their ricochet aspirations
receded past sight
and anticipated applause.
Avoiding their influence like
I avoid a bruised apple, rancid
undergrowth and go-to comforts.
It doesn't work
to alleviate the raw intensity pangs
or to revamp those dreams into something
viable, buckled-up and worthy.
I release my indulges of hope,
release a future deserving of a satisfied death
with seldom the anguish of regrets and senselessness.
I let this excellent illusion end, concede,
just breathe for the sake of it, just
wake up and do what I do, corrected,
my poverty exposed.

Crack the
Exterior, Interior
Resonance

Neither the net
or the withdrawal
will get you into its vice,
but the trick of broken dreams,
walking backwards, assuming
nothing new is possible
that will be your defeat, the pit
in the black olive that stuck in your throat,
swelled up your windpipe and laid you down.

Throw away the decadence of fear,
no matter how reasonable,
fuel yourself only on ethereal faith
even though you feel condemned,
can see no exit door or revival.

Choose God over understanding,
peace over rationality.
Smell the oil, expose the miracle rising to meet you,
pushing you on, defend its mastery and strength,
choose truth that triumphs over traditions,
penetrates every nook and cranny,
inverting, setting aright
visible appearances.

A King

Bold blood brilliance,
the tactics, the uencroachable confidence
of his glacial brutality, clemency,
making victory out of nowhere.
Odds always against him, titling one way
to be seen and the opposite way to be heard.
Swelling with passion, with genius strategies
unthought of, fertilizing the crescendo of
music chanting his praise and undeniable
sovereignty.

Introduce me, let me smell
his intake-outtake of electricity,
the absolute procurement of all his needs
through risk and never doubting his good fortune.
Let me see into his eyes
devouring like a blackhole stillness, a force
immune to resistance.
Let me witness his charm,
the slavish devotion he demands and receives
naturally.

At once crowned,
(still frenziedly restless at the centre)
then blindsided by an unexpected,
equally violent, legendary and grand
downfall.

Marsh

I walk into a forbidden marsh,
to rest from the penalty of my dreams.
I place my head on a pile of wet debris
and wait to see who or what approaches.

If everything was in line with a harmonic tune,
with the uniting truth, then my hopes
would not cling like leaches to my thighs,
reducing me with malnourishment.
I could piece together a path to travel
out of this marsh, out of the gloom
and rotting mulch.

As it is, I am overdrawn,
my bucket is cracked
and my clothes outgrown.
The wind has always scooped me into
its scarcity and a solitary translation
without recognition.
No one sees me or needs me anymore.

The marsh is my devoured saving.
The stench of what is left fills my nostrils,
reminds me of my stagnation,
is the rising gaseous force
of my obvious doom.

Maple Syrup

Today the cup is cracked,
freedom arrives lacking support
but giving time for me to strengthen enough
to make the flight and wipe the table
spotless.
Today the gift arrives
in the guise of a curse, compassion
manifesting as trauma and
either I will go mad or lighten my load
and affirm the movement finally possible,
outshine my fears, avoiding the scurrying ants
in the pantry, close the door and find alternate
sources of food, incapable of infestation,
pure as well-water, pure as God's love always is
when I accept it, when I accept all I own is a choice
of faith or cynicism, when I welcome
the hand of the one who sent me,
hold that hand, following and wanting
for nothing more.

Gift

Rebellion innate in the seed,
at the start, acknowledging
the culpability of the
the acceptable unjust, of landing
where others crawl, and still others, soar.

I cracked, eager for righteousness
but ungrateful.
You stood beside me, never wavering
or surrendering to anxiety. Your devotion
surpassed any generosity I've ever known.
Where others have abandoned or made
light of the news, offering
no humanity or understanding -
you alone held my hand,
shadowed me through hospital halls,
nourishing me through my despair
and the savage aftermath of failure.

There is nothing to be gained from
that gruesome experience, but your triumphant love,
that you were there and remain here
as my refuge, an anointment of great mercy,
a lasting antidote.

Rabbit

Broken longing
healed in the eyes
of a tender receiver, blessed
by mercy and the promise of perpetual drink.
Soft, silky warmth beside me
fragile and more precious than
any perfectly-cut gemstone.

Faith once mangled now restored
to a richer glory than introduced before.
Solitude in communion - God inside
a gentle touch, mutual bond and loneliness appeased.

Sweet waters of fate receive me,
my neck is stretched high,
my arms are a basket.

Let the unassuming reign,
place me secure in this place
where the private and the meagre
are honoured, quietly
declared yours.

If

If we live
through this hangman's touch,
outrun this heatwave and find
an oasis in spite of the odds,
then we will be sealed
in the summer of our belonging.

We will take only what we are given
to own, dress up occasionally, mostly
be charmed by sweet and simple delights.

If we survive
the devouring vultures, the
vanity of self-punishment and
the unbreakable natural law,
then our breadbasket will be
overflowing with leftovers,
our hearts will be still in the peace
of eternal love, loving this day and the next
as lovers do, happy to serve,
happy to fill the bathtub
and soak.

You Heard Me

You heard me speaking
and you shook the floor,
loosening the dust and devastating
sadness until that floor
was dismantled and replaced
by a stronger, easier-to-clean
platform, until the miracle
rose unpolluted in a continual
swelling, sinking the darkness for good,
calling brother to sister to the truth
of your perfect temple, worshiping the work
of love, relieving the weight of chaos.

You heard me and I know you are perfect,
more real than the burrowing fears inside my head,
more powerful than the churning sickness of
anxiety that overtakes my gut, overtakes and takes
me away from you.

You who heard me,
through paralysis and poison,
through my weak overtures, ripped away
my unhealthy accumulations, cleansing
my desires that missed the mark,
until I saw and committed
to one voice, one priority, listening.

Zen Virgin

This killer yoke
was pieced together from another century,
enforcing brutal labour,
swollen joints from overload
and depression swamping the upper ground.

You know it has always driven the hunt,
from your parents' childhood homes
in Indian monsoons and Polish Februarys -
dishwashing, factory working, 4 a.m. typing,
deciding to plot an unexpected ending,
yet still, following form.

You know you can get out only
if you stop defending all of its creation, only
if you drain your devotion and broaden what
you are and are not permitted to be.

You can get out, flashing, golden-sea eyes
flashing and leaping in celebration of the door touched
and opened, the re-wiring that burns every wire
and sets down the players and the playing board.

Do this emptying.
Trust it is done and it will be done.

You can hold your shoes in one hand
and your truth in another,
put on those shoes and yield to a direction
unprecedented.

Mark it down

Great joys approach
like weeping harmonies in music,
relief in the course-correction,
astonishment in the manifold beauty.
Decorations placed around the table.
Declarations for devotion riveting
through the backyard garden where
everything overflows with abundance,
is a tapestry of young blood frolicking.
Shared surges of strong faith between us,
because our love is never ending
because the loudest boom has exploded
altering the vibration here and forever,
a higher octave, a mountain sailed over,
a vision walked into, gallant and kind -
welcoming, offering
to fully bathe our bodies, open a fortune box
so we can step away from restrictions, step into
a beautiful anticipation.

Pasture

I can see my mind in victory
over the clinging contaminating thoughts
that used to spiral in a vigorous loop
through my days even when in joy,
even when hearing a tambourine tune
rise up, happy and fresh.
Now those thoughts struggle to stand,
abandoned in a desert vast
and widowed. Dehydrated unto death
they sometimes whisper, but barely have a hold
or exert a reasonable authority.

My shame has packed its belongings and left.
My self-pity has reduced its wound
to a pin-prick along with my bitterness.
Gratitude is the only dream worth feeding.
I will feed it and not be overwhelmed
or react to desperate hungry
rumblings, not react in desperation
to what is lacking on the canvas, on the alter,
or in my understanding and this growing surrender.

Learning

Because I said
it was not enough,
the emptiness came
like a hard beat plummeting
me into doom.
Because I cared to record
each pain, betrayal and fracture,
I could not walk fast and glinting,
dragged back and down.
Because I lost my worship,
I lost my joy and the heat of life
that inspires.

Because I took heed of these pitfalls
and take one section of the day at a time
to do and explore both service and favour,
I am uncovering a mosaic beneath my feet,
smelling scents I thought disappeared with my youth.
Because I keep the rituals that keep me sane,
in storm or shade, I pray more than I dream
and when I dream it is about abstractions,
about tree branches, blankets, about
the hair's breadth distance between sea and stars.

Immersed

This shift is gracious
like a runaway found and comforted.
Disguised as an axe-lop,
as a callous reduction of earned respect,
this shift is permission
for exploration, expansion into
clear waters, tickled by the fish seen
circling below.

I can greet those fish,
each one as an individual, bend my body
and enjoy the details of their scales,
the space between their fins, and their lips,
thick and sometimes scarred
by hooks or other near-disasters.

I can give up my burden, my self-attention
and observe, appreciate their maneuvering
between my calves and shins, over my toes,
curious at these fleshy stumps of mine,
appearing in their home.

I can tell them I am friendly,
a friend, not here to make a disturbance.
I can be motionless for a while, because of the shift.
Because of the shift I am opened, receiving gladly
each delicate undulating swerve,
each nibble, sway.

Outline

Too bad you got burned
on the spell of worldly accomplishments
and comparison, that you fell
into the snowbank and drenched yourself through.
Friendly false eyes in the flame,
in the sweating ruthless ocean - you lost
the hand that held you to truth and the longing
for a deeper betterment.

But now you are home, proclaiming
the invisible as your building blocks - piled high
and mortared together strong against every storm.
You almost got pulled into the everlasting pit, fooled
by fool's gold, but you reached the upper edge and
lifted yourself to a safe landing.

Eat from your bowl and be grateful.
Everything you asked for is already yours.
Walk away from the party,
shake hands, give uncommitted hugs,
then read by the dim light, knowing your true riches,
knowing all that you treasure is complete, thriving
in this compact tried-and-true family
and in the landscape of your evolving solitude.

Footsteps

of a haunted lion mourning
her lost young. In a cage,
another brow folded in grief
and grim expectation.
Entitlement massaged into the bright blank eyes
of the classless rich with their toothy smiles
and ego-feeding gestures
of generosity.

The lion is haunted, the rabbit
is caged and the mournful dog longs for kinship.
The sacred is devoured but not for long
and not forever
as joy overtakes with one relaxed touch,
one moment of complete enjoyable surrender
where nothing impure
can enter.

That moment is worth poverty, worth
the fevered greed swirling around,
spoiling the atmosphere,
tricking with false kindness and ignorance of self
that leads to chaotic manipulation.
It is worth the penalty of no security

just to combine for a few moments
with another's spirit, be grand
in such holiness, be humbled
by such rudimentary love.

Jesus in the Marrow

You arrived again, reviving
the groove, clearing
out the debris of lingering
madness and anxiety, brilliant
blazing again with your miracles,
your compassion that leaves me breathless
with joy, surges within with affection, protecting,

feeling like a did when I was a child
and my father walked with me on his shoulders
and I could see higher, further than ever before,
safe and moving, knowing
I would never be harmed, never abandoned,
knowing the freedom of a child's fearlessness,
trust in the strength of the one who loves me,
trust in the power of the one who carries me like
a queen, like someone special,
unshackling my imagination, restoring my vigour
and swoon.

You arrived again and I remember
all of it, all of your love,
dazzling, perfect, saturating
my seat at the table, overflowing.

Intertwined

Together like odours
that merge in a closed room,
blending indistinguishable,
we are continual - each the same
as the other - in plague breath, in worries,
and in peace-filled joys, hopes that restore
strength and future paths beautifully unfolding.

So we decorate inside, never letting on
how much care we give to each detail.
Truth is kind to us as we hold hands across
the sofa, smiling at each other because
there is no corruption between us, no hidden
regrets or festering resentments when we see each other
we see a gift of eternal faithfulness, a lifetime pact,
sure-footed, winged and light and rich as honey
on the tongue, as a friendship that has never betrayed
or grown stale, and a love in a constant cycle of aching,
being satiated, counting on satiation and thresholds
reached and surpassed, sensuously mastered
together, often weary, but never of each other.

Only you are my love, bound
like the stem to its flower,
and the hawk to its sharp eye.

We will give nothing to the rest
that does not join our great love,
tries to defile our green fields flowing
or make us believe in less than this miracle.

For all things of life are ours -
our veins, our holy light-strings,
intensely locked, tenderly alive.

This end

This end is an offspring
to tend to and adore,
breaking through distinctive patterns
that worked for a while, but now,
only harm.

This offspring is musical,
composing practices and prayers,
hungering for the details
to disinfect and clean.

This joy is unspoken,
activity with no burdensome description,
uninfected with expectations, obligations
or the guarding dog.

This house has been lived in,
all things that have died have died
again, deeper, and finally here, renewed.

Faith is the exact destination, lapping the plate
sparkling so all that is left is awe and mercy, digesting
simplicity in the swelling brightness before me.

I have you again like at the start
when I first witnessed your face
and hair and eyes and loved you
with a bliss that in the past
I could only steal from books but now
I owned, uniquely as my own.

Trees hang over the cliff.
Behind me is the summit.
My foolish hopes align
with divinity's commands.
Bars are dropped, lightweight like pins.
Moon and sun full, clearly visible
in the same morning sky.

Homecoming

Returning to the kelp forest
as a companion to a larger inhabitant,
as a guest to the great reef waters,
a lover of the odd and miraculous,
seduced by succulent influences,
descending then rising all in good speed.
I welcome the sand dwellers
and the tunnel diggers. I am welcomed
by the tentacled and the fanged,
and by the soft, squishy translucent floaters.
I am just another creature that eats or will be eaten,
and I relish in this environment of unquestioning acceptance
my minuscule place.
I ride the back of the bottom feeder. I find my own
way through the caves, avoiding the high price
of this liberty.
I have returned and I am not leaving
for a more agreeable, less authentic reality.
My form is older, broken, degenerating, but
I feel it again, my nerves,
secret sensations, glorious intensity,
awakening like during the first fall,
like the first time waiting
to being caught, irrevocably
saved.

Jesus Holds

Nudging, pushing,
foot-tripping to
kindle a dream that
runs publicized on every
channel, uttering its happy fortune,
lined up with divine commands.

The abyss is an arrow shot right through,
splitting what doesn't belong away from
the thriving harvest. If you try to
cross it, you will fall into it,
for the health of the harvest cannot be soiled
with past inclusions.

Promises made are finding
fruition, and greed and bitterness
have diffused into a calm surrender
to the unknown.

This friendship lasts forever,
it does not let go
in the wake of an attaching darkness.
It banishes anger, exposes
scars covering the face
and under layered clothes.

This friendship demands no other
connection as strong as its own,

peels away the scaly scabs inside the ears,
adds up all dividends, then pays out without
scratching or lashing
the spinning inner sacred core.

Not a Mirage

  Ambushed, held hostage, then forgotten,
discarded, starved and too weak
to move. I find myself in a dead forest
that was burned by a fire a few years ago -
just sprouts of trees and a few ants trailing
the chewed-up ground.
  I will find a cabin to rest in and get warm,
then find food in that cabin and rejuvenate.
I will not think of them (those who took me)
more than I have to. I will not
devote my energy
to bitterness but fasten myself
to thoughts of a future where freedom
is mine and I am not obliged to sleep
my nights in a mite-infested bed or
pull at my hair-strands
in boredom.
  My burden is unloaded,
my shackles are far away
after so many decades.
It will take commitment to shine
in order to shine, but I will shine.
  Near a country river
I will make my home, remain
tied to a promise like a covenant devoid
of self-pity, return to joy
as though never captured, never broken.

Against Gravity

He sings because he is song,
essence-song -
potent life, potent death forever.
He dreams salubrious dreams,
fatter at the core and needle-hard all around.
He lost the need for enchantment
and exhibition. The inveterate intensity
within him is mastered, absorbed into his every cell.
It is not that he is better, only more genuine
in his connection, metaphors advancing,
infiltrating his pulse.

He knows because he is wild, dangerously free.
Break him with poverty and he will break every rule.
He will burst into flight, dancing against gravity,
against a blood-moon.
Tin-foil wrap him into a put-upon routine
and he will make music from the crackling -
laid out flat, pressed down,
he will transform his form, rising
whole in an inspired reverie.

About the Author

Allison Grayhurst is a member of the League of Canadian Poets. Four of her poems were nominated for "Best of the Net" in 2015/2018, and one eight-part story-poem was nominated for "Best of the Net" in 2017. She has over 1,375 poems published in more than 525 international journals and anthologies.

Her book *Somewhere Falling* was published by Beach Holme Publishers, a Porcepic Book, in Vancouver in 1995. Since then she has published twenty other books of poetry and five collections with Edge Unlimited Publishing. Prior to the publication of Somewhere Falling she had a poetry book published, *Common Dream*, and four chapbooks published by The Plowman.
Her poetry chapbook The *River is Blind* was published by Ottawa publisher above/ground press December 2012. In 2014 her chapbook *Surrogate Dharma* was published by Kind of a Hurricane Press, Barometric Pressures Author Series. In 2015, her book *No Raft – No Ocean* was published by Scars Publications.

Her book *Make the Wind* was published in 2016 by Scars Publications.

As well, her book *Trial and Witness – selected poems*, was published in 2016 by Creative Talents Unleashed (CTU Publishing Group).

More recently, her book *Tadpoles Find the Sun* was published by Cyberwit, August 2020.

In 2020, her work was translated into Chinese and published in "Rendition of International Poetry Quarterly" and in "Poetry Hall".

In 2018, her book *Sight at Zero*, was listed #34 on CBC's "Your Ultimate Canadian Poetry List".

Collaborating with Allison Grayhurst on the lyrics, Vancouver-based singer/songwriter/musician Diane Barbarash has transformed eight of Allison Grayhurst's poems into songs, creating a full album. "River – Songs from the poetry of Allison Grayhurst" released October 2017.

Allison Grayhurst is a vegan for the animals. She lives in Toronto with her family. She also sculpts, working with clay; www.allisongrayhurst.com